better together*

*This book is best read together, grownup and kid.

a kids book about ™

a kids book about™ LEADERSHIP

by Orion Jean

**a
kids
book
about**™

A Kids Book About books are available online:
www.akidsbookabout.com

To share your stories, ask questions, or inquire about bulk
purchases (schools, libraries, and nonprofits), please use
the following email address:

hello@akidsbookabout.com

ISBN: 978-1-953955-07-4

Designed by Duke Stebbins
Edited by Emma Wolf

For my loving parents, who have taught me more about how to lead than anyone I know.

Intro

I want you to close your eyes (well, kind of, but not really, because I want you to keep reading), and imagine this...

What if EVERY kid knew they had the power to become a leader? At the age of 9, I discovered the leader inside of me, and with my newfound superpower, decided to spread kindness throughout the world to help others. How would the world be different if EVERY kid unearthed the leader inside of them? The possibilities are endless for what kids of any age can accomplish in this world. Don't get me wrong, I'm not saying that every kid HAS to be the next CEO or world leader, but they can begin showing their leadership in small (and sometimes BIG) ways that truly matter to them. And who knows—with a little work and time, today's kids could become some of the greatest leaders we have ever seen!

I hope this book sparks a conversation about this superpower that lies within all kids and inspires them to be the next changemakers of the world.

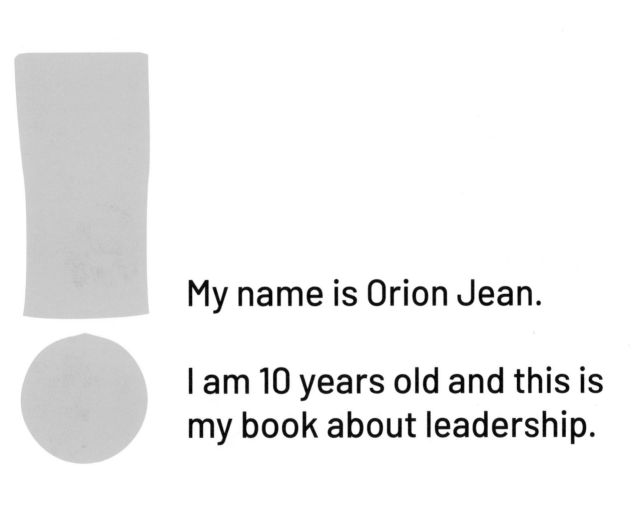

My name is Orion Jean.

I am 10 years old and this is
my book about leadership.

Let me tell you a bit about myself:

My favorite foods are sprinkles, marshmallows, and anything fried.

(I also think a fried marshmallow with sprinkles on it would be *perfect*!)

I love *The Lion King*—I could watch that movie over and over.

I am also a pretty big stickler for grammar.

And I'm here today because I'm a leader.

I'm also here because I know

you are a leader, too...

**you just might not see it
in yourself yet.**

Even though I'm a kid,
I've led others
(kids AND grownups)
in really awesome things,
like donating over 600 toys
to a hospital, and over
100,000 meals to
people in need.

What do You think of

when you think of leadership?

To me, leadership is not just about managing people...

it's about guiding people with **kindness** and **confidence**.

Leading people in kindness means you don't just tell people,

"HeY!

You have to go be kind NOW!"

It's helping people and showing them ways to be kind.

IT can LOOK LIKE:

- asking your parents how you can help out around the house

- babysitting your siblings

- cheering on your friends when they aren't feeling confident

- eating lunch with someone who you notice is sitting alone

- offering to show a new student around your school

- sending a personal note

You have to lead by example
so others follow. And don't forget,

when you lead with kindness,

EVERY-
BODY
WINS.

As a leader, it's also important to follow through.

So many people get these great ideas but never act on them.

That's why having a team is so great!

Because you'll have lots of other people to push you toward accomplishing your goals!

Having a team is a

HU

part of leadership.

It's important to make sure your team feels needed in the conversation.

No matter what decision you make, your team should be involved and everyone should feel like they have a purpose that matters.

I won a speech contest when I was 9. The theme was kindness, and with the prize money I received, I started the Race to Kindness, which is about donating resources to people in need.

I've managed to help thousands of people, and I couldn't have done all that without working together, with my friends and family, **as a** TEAM!

It's important that everyone can work together in a way where you can compromise,* get stuff done, and allow each person to have a say.

*A compromise is an agreement that may not be what each person wants but works best for everyone.

Something else about working with a team is that everybody has different strengths and weaknesses.

For example...

SOME——TIMES

I'm impatient.

I like getting new projects started, but from time to time, it can be hard to be patient all the way through to the end of a plan.

Thankfully, my mom is great at being patient with both my brother and me.

SOME — TIMES

I'm indecisive.

I like thinking out all of my decisions, but I can get stuck in my head trying to make the perfect choice.

Luckily for me, my dad is really great at thinking about who we're serving.

When I'm not feeling confident, he's always there to guide me toward making a choice I can feel proud of.

SOME — TIMES

I'm pessimistic.

I tend to consider every possible outcome for a given situation, and that means I can concentrate on the negative side too much.

But, my parents always make sure I'm able to see the silver lining in things and focus on the brighter side.

They always lift me up so that I can get right back into the swing of things.

The truth is, being a leader can seem overwhelming.

Believe me! Trying to bring in enough food to feed thousands of people was no small task!

It can sometimes seem like saying "**no thanks**" would be a lot easier, and I could go on for hours with countless excuses kids make as to why they don't think they can be leaders.

"I don't have the resources to do this. I'm not old enough. I'm afraid to start. What if I make the wrong decision? What if I fail? It's too hard! I can barely lead myself...

How am I supposed to lead other people? What if I just want to focus on getting through the day? Does leadership involve me giving away my food? My time? My toys?"

I can confidently say leading is going to be a little bit hard, and you're going to have to give away some of your time to do it.

But all you really need to get started

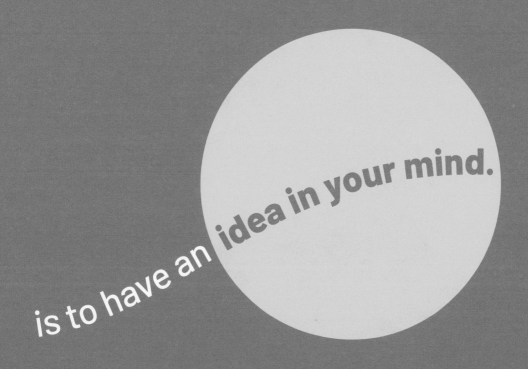
is to have an idea in your mind.

You can still be a leader even if...

you're nervous, you have doubts,

you don't feel brave every day,

or you don't know where to begin.

Just share your **idea** with an adult, and start small.

You could donate 5 toys to a local hospital, or visit a food bank and drop off some of your favorite foods for people to enjoy.

When you know that people need something more than you do, THAT'S when you have to be willing to give.

There's more than one way
to be a leader.

You can do small things
and big ones too!

Kids like you and me
do big things every day.

You just need to carry yourself—
and maybe, carry others—
with kindness.

Your ideas and your thoughts matter.

Even if you feel small you can influence just **1 person**.

Maybe it's... your mom, your dad, your sibling, your neighbor, your classmate, or your friend.

And that one person can influence someone in their own lives.

causing a ripple effect, which all together

can change the world!

Kids may not know everything,
but we can worry less about
having everything figured out,
and focus on listening
and growing every day.

So one day,
when we have big roles to play,
we can lead in a good and kind way,
and make sure that no matter who
we are or where we come from,
we inspire others to lead.

Anyone can become a leader.

Even

Outro

Grownups, this book is as much for you as it is for kids. After reading this, I hope that you too feel inspired to find new ways to lead in your life and support your kid in their leadership journey. If so, here are a few things to keep in mind:

1. If your kid comes to you with a leadership idea, help them figure out the best ways to make it happen. Encouraging them to focus on the "why" will help them stay motivated, even when things get hard.

2. Help them identify and celebrate their strengths and teach them to see their weaknesses as opportunities to grow and team up with others. Remind them that YOU are a part of their team and that you will work together to accomplish their goal.

3. Lead by example and allow your kids to see you being a leader. Share your own challenges with them and show them how you've overcome those obstacles.

The path to leadership is different for everyone. But if we can encourage kids to get started, it can help them discover more about their superpower and give them the confidence to lead anytime and anywhere. And that just may be the secret to changing the world!

find more kids books about

belonging, feminism, creativity, money, depression, failure, gratitude, adventure, cancer, body image, and school shootings.

akidsbookabout.com

notes

share
your read*

*Tell somebody, post a photo, or give this book away to share what you care about.

@akidsbookabout